I0388789

PRAYING IN THE SPIRIT

Praying always with all prayer and supplication in the Spirit, and watching thereunto with all perseverance and supplication for all saints.

Ephesians 6:18 *KJV*

by
Franklin N. Abazie

Praying In the Spirit
COPYRIGHT 2016 BY Franklin N Abazie
ISBN: 978-1-94513304-6

All right reserved. This book or any portion thereof may not be reproduced or used in any manner whatsoever without the express written permission of the publisher, except for the use of brief quotations in a book review. All Bible quotes are from King James Version and others as noted.

Published by: F N ABAZIE PUBLISHING HOUSE—aka, Empowerment Bookstore

That I may publish with the voice of thanksgiving and tell of all thy wondrous works.
Psalms 26:7

To order additional copies, wholesales or booking call:
the Church office (973-372-7518)
or Empowerment Bookstore Hotline (973-393-8518)

Worship address:
343 Sanford Avenue, Newark, New Jersey 07106
Administrative Head Office address:
33 Schley Street Newark New Jersey 07112
Email: pastorfranknto@yahoo.com
Website www.fnabaziehealingministries.org
Publishing House: www.fnabaziepublishinghouse.org

This book is a production of F N Abazie Publishing House. A publication Arms of Miracle of God Ministries 2016.
First Edition

CONTENTS

THE MANDATE OF THE COMMISSION......................iv
ARMS OF THE COMMISSION......................................v
INTRODUCTION..vi
CHAPTER 1
What is Prayer..1
CHAPTER 2
The Tongue of Angels..15
CHAPTER 3
The Forces of the Spirit...22
CHAPTER 4
The Help of the Holy Spirit...34
CHAPTER 5
Prayer of Salvation..61
CHAPTER 6
About the Author...70

THE MANDATE OF THE COMMISSION

"The moment is due to impact your world through the revival of the healing & miracle ministry of Jesus Christ of Nazareth.

"I am sending you to restore health unto thee and I will heal thee of thy wounds, said the Lord of Host."

ARMS OF THE COMMISSION

1) F N Abazie Ministries—Miracle of God Ministries (Miracle Chapel Intl)

2) F N Abazie TV Ministries: Global Television Ministry Outreach

3) F N Abazie Radio Ministries: Radio Broadcasting Outreach

4) F N Abazie Publishing House: Book Publication

5) F N Abazie Bible School: also called Word of Healing Bible School (W.O.H.B.S.)

6) F N Abazie Evangelistic Ass: Miracle of God Ministries: Global Crusade

7) Empowerment Bookstore: Book distribution

8) F N Abazie Helping Hands: Meeting the Help of the Needy Worldwide

9) F N Abazie Disaster Recovery Mission: Global Disaster Recovery

10) F N Abazie Prison Ministry: Prison Ministry For All Convicts "Second Chance"

Some of our ministry arms are awaiting the appointed time to commence.

INTRODUCTION

> *Wherefore let him that speaketh in*
> *an unknown tongue pray that he may interpret.*
> *For if I pray in an unknown tongue,*
> *my spirit prayeth, but my understanding*
> *is unfruitful. What is it then? I will pray*
> *with the spirit, and I will pray*
> *with the understanding also:*
> *I will sing with the spirit, and I will sing*
> *with the understanding also.*
> **1 Corinthians 14:13-15**

In these dreadful days we live in, praying in the spirit is of neccessity. So many of us pray often, but how many of us are really **praying in the spirit**.

There are different levels and dimensions of prayer. Every now and then most of us will mutter a few words for five to 10 minutes and we claim we just prayed. In my definition, prayer is an invitation that gives God the authorization to intervene in the affairs of man.

Prayer determines your level of command in the realms of the spirit. As long as you can pray feverently in the spirit for at least three to five hours, you are on your way into breakthrough. Most of us pastors and apostles wish for a great church, but nothing will happen until we pray. The Bible said Paul planted Appolo's waters, but it is God who brings the increase.

And it came to pass about an eight days after these sayings, he took Peter and John and James, and went up into a mountain to pray.
And as he prayed, the fashion of his countenance was altered, and his raiment was white and glistering. And, behold, there talked with him two men, which were Moses and Elias:
Luke 9:28-30

Prayer is a daily necessity. If we must survive in these evil days, we must begin to call on God more often than we used to.

Evening, and morning, and at noon, will I pray, and cry aloud: and he shall hear my voice
Psalms 55:17

Now when Daniel knew that the writing was signed, he went into his house; and his windows being open in his chamber toward Jerusalem, he kneeled upon his knees three times a day, and prayed, and gave thanks before his God, as he did aforetime.
Daniel 6:10

David and Daniel in the above scriptures prayed three times in one day. It is time for the church of God to wake up and pray. A recent study proved that an average pastor prayed only ten minutes in one week. We must learn how to pray often. Prayer is our only communication channel to talk to God. Every time you pray in the spirit you step out of humanity into divinty.

Jesus Christ of Nazareth taught his disciples how to pray.

*And it came to pass, that, as he was praying
in a certain place, when he ceased,
one of his disciples said unto him,
Lord, teach us to pray, as John also taught his disciples.
And he said unto them, When ye pray, say,
Our Father which art in heaven, Hallowed be thy name.
Thy kingdom come. Thy will be done, as in heaven,
so in earth. Give us day by day our daily bread. And forgive
us our sins; for we also forgive every one that is indebted to
us. And lead us not into temptation; but deliver us from evil.*
Luke 11:1-4

Message Bible put it this way:

*One day he was praying in a certain place. When he
finished, one of his disciples said, "Master, teach us to pray
just as John taught his disciples."
So he said, "When you pray, say,
Father,
Reveal who you are.
Set the world right.
Keep us alive with three square meals.
Keep us forgiven with you and forgiving others.
Keep us safe from ourselves and the Devil."*
Luke 11:1-4

This book has been written out of my love for the kingdom of God and his righteousness and out of my love for prayer.

As a man of prayer I have listen a read testimonies of prayers from my living mentors like David Yonggi Cho who prayed for seven to eight hours daily asking God to send the Holy Spirit to grow his church. To my late mentors like John and Charles Wesley who said it appear like God will do nothing untill somebody prays, for me to conclude that it is prayer that establishes any church gathering or fellowship.

Prayer moves the spirit of God, prayer brings God into the scene. The great Queen Victoria of Scotland once said that I fear nothing but the prayers of John Knox.

And he went a little farther, and fell on his face, and prayed, saying, O my Father, if it be possible, let this cup pass from me: nevertheless not as I will, but as thou wilt. And he cometh unto the disciples, and findeth them asleep, and saith unto Peter, What, could ye not watch with me one hour? Watch and pray, that ye enter not into temptation: the spirit indeed is willing, but the flesh is weak.
Matthew 26:39-41

It is prayer that sustains the physical and spiritual life of the believer. It is prayer that generates favor from God. We all must not slack from praying. We all must rise up as intercessors and begin to deploy the power of the attorney in the name of Jesus Christ. We must pull the trigger against the devil's wiles and schemes by the blood of Jesus.

Jesus said....

And whatsoever ye shall ask in my name,
that will I do, that the Father may be glorified in the Son.
If ye shall ask any thing in my name, I will do it.
John 14:13-14

If you desire to pray in the spirit, you must take your time out to read these books.]

Come with me as I explain my insight on the subject of praying in the spirit.

HAPPY READING!!!

Because we cannot pray in the spirit without the help of the HOLY SPIRIT, I have highlighted how to receive the Holy Spirit.

HIGHLIGHTS

HOW TO RECEIVE THE HOLY SPIRIT

REPENT

Every time we are willing to "REPENT," GOD will dispatch the HOLY SPIRIT to **restore our lives**—REPENTANCE GRANTS RESTORATION.

Whenever we repent of our sins, God is excited to help our infirmities. "*If my people, which are called by my name, shall humble themselves, and pray, and seek my face, and turn from their wicked ways; then will I hear from heaven, and will forgive their sin, and will heal their land.*" (2 Chronicles 7:14)

Men and brethren, what shall we do?
Then Peter said unto them, Repent, and be baptized
every one of you in the name of Jesus Christ for the
remission of sins, and ye shall receive
the gift of the Holy Ghost.
Acts 2:37-38

Repentance is the access code into praying in the spirit. Genuine repentance is the access code to navigate easily when praying in the spirit.

SALVATION

The word "salvation" means deliverance from sin, sickness, poverty, affliction, shame. etc. If you have not truly confessed Jesus Christ as your lord and savior. There is nothing the Father can do for you. We cannot pray in the spirit if we have not received genuine salvation. No man or woman can deny the work of salvation. Salvation means deliverance from sin and redemption by the blood of Jesus Christ.

FAITH

And the prayer of faith shall save the sick, and the Lord shall raise him up; and if he have committed sins, they shall be forgiven him.
James 5:15

Unless otherwise stated, as far as I know, it is the **prayer of faith that saves the sick**. Our Prayer must be mixed with our Faith. The Bible says as the body without the SPIRIT is dead, so FAITH without WORKS is dead also. For our PRAYERS to be effective, it must be mixed with our FAITH. "*For verily I say unto you, That whosoever shall say unto this mountain, Be thou removed, and be thou cast into the sea; and shall not doubt in his heart, but shall believe that those things which he saith shall come to pass; he shall have whatsoever he saith.*" (Mark 11:23)

DECISION

Before you pray either in the spirit or in tongue, you must decide on *what* to pray about. *"And it came to pass, that, as he was praying in a certain place, when he ceased, one of his disciples said unto him, Lord, teach us to pray, as John also taught his disciples. And he said unto them, When ye pray, say, Our Father which art in heaven, Hallowed be thy name. Thy kingdom come. Thy will be done, as in heaven, so in earth. Give us day by day our daily bread. And forgive us our sins; for we also forgive every one that is indebted to us. And lead us not into temptation; but deliver us from evil."* (Luke 11:1-2)

We must make up our mind before we even **pray**. DECISIONS are the wheels of destiny. We either ride into ETERNITY—or into HELL FIRE. We must all make up our minds concerning HEAVEN. The only time to take advantage of our lives is now that we are alive. *"For he saith, I have heard thee in a time accepted, and in the day of salvation have I succoured thee: behold, now is the accepted time; behold, now is the day of salvation."* (2 Corinthians 6:2)

For the grave cannot praise thee, death cannot celebrate thee: they that go down into the pit cannot hope for thy truth. The living, the living, he shall praise thee, as I do this day: the father to the children shall make known thy truth.
Isaiah 38:18-19

PRAYER

But ye beloved, building up your selves on your most holy faith, praying in the Holy Ghost.
Jude 1:20

The Bible says, *"Likewise the Spirit also helpeth our infirmities; for we know not what we should pray for as we ought: but the Spirit itself maketh intercession for us with groaning which cannot be uttered."* (Romans 8:26)

Prayer is so vital in our lives, because anytime we pray in tongues, we provoke the presence of the Holy Spirit into our lives. It is the Holy Spirit that grants our Spirit Man assurance and rest from any prevailing trouble. *"The Spirit itself beareth witness with our spirit, that we are the children of God."* (Romans 8:16)

PRAYER POINT TO ACTIVATE THE PRESENCE OF THE HOLY SPIRIT

1) Holy Spirit, reveal yourself to me, in the name of Jesus.

2) Holy Spirit, crush every daily habit of sin, in the name of Jesus.

3) Holy Spirit, become my companion today, in the name of Jesus.

4) Holy Spirit, grant me access, in the name of Jesus.

5) Power of God, grant me the *grace* to live right for Jesus Christ.

6) Hand of God, deliver me from sin, in the name of Jesus.

7) Fire of God, burn every sinful thoughts from my mind, in the name of Jesus.

8) I proclaim authority over every prevailing sin in my life, in Jesus name.

9) I destroy every root of sin in my life, in Jesus name.

10) Sin shall not have dominion over my life, in the

name of Jesus.

11) Lord God, emphasize genuine repentance over my Spirit man, in the name of Jesus

12) Holy Spirit, revive and rekindle your fire of revival inside of me, in the name of Jesus.

13) Power of God, hijack the controlling forces oppressing my life, in the name of Jesus.

14) Blood of Jesus, take over my life, in the name of Jesus.

15) O Lord, baptize me with the gift of the Holy Spirit.

16) Holy Spirit, breathe afresh upon my life, in the name of Jesus.

17) Holy Spirit, take possession of my will, in the name of Jesus.

18) Holy Spirit, make yourself real to me, in the name of Jesus.

19) Holy Spirit, fan your revival fire upon my life, in the name of Jesus.

CHAPTER 1
WHAT IS PRAYER?

Prayer is listening and talking to God in a dialogue. It is **communicating** to the **spirit of God** with **revrence, respect** and **humility**. So many of us **pray** all the time without getting results.

Although too many bible scholars has made so many definition about **praying in the spirit**. All access into praying in the spirit is by the help of the Holy Spirit. If the Holy Ghost grants you utterance, then we can pray in the spirit.

Likewise the Spirit also helpeth our infirmities:
for we know not what we should pray for as we ought:
but the Spirit itself maketh intercession for us with
groanings which cannot be uttered
Romans 8:26

Oftentimes some addicted church folks pretend to be in the **spirit**. Whenever you are in the **spirit**, the **Holy Spirit** brings a conviction over that circumstance.

There must be order in the house of **God**. Do not burst into tongues when the Holy Spirit is not leading you. I have seen men and women moved by the Holy Spirit. I've also seen men and women moved by their own zealous fleshy nature. It's the Holy Spirit who teaches us all things, including **praying in the spirit**.

*But the comforter, which is the Holy Ghost,
whom the Father will send in my name,
he shall teach you all things, and bring
all things to your remembrance,
whatsoever I have said unto you.*
John 14:26

The Holy Spirit as the comforter, Jesus himself needed him most, to strengthen him before his death. The Bible says how God anointed Jesus of Nazareth with the Holy Ghost and with power; who went about doing good, and healing all that were oppressed of the devil; for God was with him.

The Holy Spirit is the comforter. Jesus said, *"I will not leave you comfortless: I will come to you."* (See John 14:26) Hence, Jesus empowered his disciples when he finally came back shortly before his ascension into heaven.

*For he that speaketh in an unknown tongue speaketh
not unto men, but unto God: for no man understandeth
him; howbeit in the spirit he speaketh mysteries.
But he that prophesieth speaketh unto men to
edification, and exhortation, and comfort. He that speaketh in an unknown tongue edifieth himself;
but he that prophesieth edifieth the church.
I would that ye all spake with tongues but rather that ye
prophesied: for greater is he that prophesieth than he
that speaketh with tongues, except he interpret, that the
church may receive edifying. Now, brethren, if I come*

Chapter 1 — What Is Prayer?

unto you speaking with tongues, what shall I profit you, except I shall speak to you either by revelation, or by knowledge, or by prophesying, or by doctrine? And even things without life giving sound, whether pipe or harp, except they give a distinction in the sounds, how shall it be known what is piped or harped? For if the trumpet give an uncertain sound, who shall prepare himself to the battle? So likewise ye, except ye utter by the tongue words easy to be understood, how shall it be known what is spoken? for ye shall speak into the air. There are, it may be, so many kinds of voices in the world, and none of them is without signification. Therefore if I know not the meaning of the voice, I shall be unto him that speaketh a barbarian, and he that speaketh shall be a barbarian unto me. Even so ye, forasmuch as ye are zealous of spiritual gifts, seek that ye may excel to the edifying of the church. Wherefore let him that speaketh in an unknown tongue pray that he may interpret. For if I pray in an unknown tongue, my spirit prayeth, but my understanding is unfruitful. What is it then? I will pray with the spirit, and I will pray with the understanding also: I will sing with the spirit, and I will sing with the understanding also. Else when thou shalt bless with the spirit, how shall he that occupieth the room of the unlearned say Amen at thy giving of thanks, seeing he understandeth not what thou sayest?
2 Corinthians 14:2-16

Whenever we speak in tongue, there must be an interpretation.

> *Who is he that saith, and it cometh to pass,*
> *when the Lord commandeth it not? .*
> **Lamentation 3:37**

It is an abomination to lie against the **Holy Spirit.**

WHAT IS SIN?

One man said S.I.N means Satan Identification Number. I do not disagree, but it is incomplete.

> *Fools make a mock at sin:*
> *but among the righteous there is favour.*
> **Proverbs 14:9**

In my own definition, sin is disobeying God's words and commandments. Every time you operate outside of the commandment of God, you are committing sin. *He that committeth sin is of the devil; for the devil sinneth from the beginning. For this purpose the son of God was manifested that he might destroy the works of the devil.* (1 John 3:8)

> *The evil bow before the good.*
> **Proverbs 14:19**

The Bible says that judgment shall start in the house of God. Oftentimes, we sin against the Holy Spirit by pretending to be **praying in the spirit.** It is either you are in the **spirit**—or you are not in the **spirit.**

WHO IS A SINNER?

The sacrifice of the wicked is an abomination to the Lord: but the prayer of the upright is his delight. The way of the wicked is an abomination unto the Lord: but he loveth him that followeth after righteousness
Proverbs 15:8-9

We are all sinners, if the truth be told. We are only trying to live a **righteous life**. *"Doing righteousness, makes us righteous."* (1 John 3:7) Only Jesus Chris knew no sin. *"For he hath made him to be sin for us, who knew no sin; that we might be made the righteousness of God in him."* (2 Corinthians 5:21)

Examine yourselves, whether ye be in the faith; prove your own selves. Know ye not your own selves, how that Jesus Christ is in you, except ye be reprobates?
2 Corinthians 13:5

Although most faith people live in denial about the work of the flesh, from my own scriptural understanding, everyone operating within the scope of Galatians 5:20-21 is classified as a sinner.

Now the works of the flesh are manifest, which are these; Adultery, fornication, uncleanness, lasciviousness, idolatry, witchcraft, hatred, variance, emulations, wrath, strife, seditions, heresies, envyings, murders, drunkenness, revellings, and such like: of the which I tell you before, as I have also told you in time past, that they which do such things shall not inherit the kingdom of God.
Galatians 5:20-21

Further supporting scripture…

But the fearful, and unbelieving, and the abominable, and murderers, and whoremongers, and sorcerers, and idolaters, and all liars, shall have their part in the lake which burneth with fire and brimstone: which is the second death.
Revelation 21:8

WHO, THEREFORE, IS A SINNER?

1) The Lazy Man: It is sinful for any able-bodied man or woman to fold their hands and make themselves beggars. The Bible says, *"the sluggard will not plow by reason of the cold; therefore shall he beg in harvest, and have nothing."* (Proverbs 20:4) In my own understanding, laziness is a sin. *For even when we were with you, this we commanded you, that if any would not work, neither should he eat.* (2 Thessalonians 3:10) Covenant mentality demands that we all understand that God has done His part over our lives.

Jesus said I must work. It is dignified for every believer to earn money through the work of their hands—although most lazy people live in denial and tend to blame someone else. Nevertheless, Godliness demands that we take absolute responsibility for the outcome of our lives.

2) Unbelievers: In my view, all that have not acknowledged Jesus Christ as Lord and savior are sinners. The Bible says *God heareth not sinners*. Without contradiction, all unbelievers live in a sinful lifestyle. Unless God has mercy, most unbelievers will not make eternity in heaven.

3) Liars: All liars are sinners before the Almighty God. Lying is a very serious sin, simply because it leads to poverty and shame. Lying decays great destiny and erodes potential future. Someone who I know very well lies so much to themselves, they became a beggar by paralyzing their future and frustrating the will of God over their life.

HOW DO I COME OUT OF SIN?

You must ***REPENT*** & ***CONFESS*** & ***PROCLAIM*** THE LORD JESUS CHRIST.

The word says as many as received him, to them gave He power to become the sons of God. Even to them that believe on his name.

To qualify for divine visitation, do the following (with sincerity):

1) *Acknowledge* that you are a sinner and that He died for you. (Romans 3:23)

2) *Repent of your sins*. (Acts 3:19, Luke 13:5, 2 Peter 3:9)

3) *Believe in your heart* that Jesus died for your sin. (Romans 10:10)

4) *Confess Jesus as the Lord over your life.* (Romans 10:10, Acts 2:21)

Now repeat this Prayer after me—

Say Lord Jesus, I accept you today, as my Lord and my savior, forgive me of my sins wash me with your blood. Right now, I believe, I am sanctified, I am save, I am free, I am free from the Power of sin to serve the Lord Jesus. Thank you Lord for saving me. Amen.

Congratulations.

YOU ARE NOW A BORN AGAIN CHRISTIAN!

Chapter 1   What Is Prayer?

STEPS TO OVERCOME THE LIFESTYLE OF SIN

FAITH

No one will overcome any sinful lifestyle without faith. Faith is the catalyst that will push you out of sin. Most prevailing controlling forces will not retreat unless the spirit of faith comes into play. Unless you develop faith, controlling forces have power to prevail. Therefore, develop faith that will crush all prevailing remote control forces. I see your faith bringing you deliverance over that prevailing lustful situation.

DECISIONS

All evil forces know when you make up your mind. In 2006, I found myself in a difficult challenge within my life and it took faith and a decision in 2008 to overcome it. In your lifetime decisions are vital keys to remain in the flight of success and excellence. Decisions are the pillars to determine the outcome of your life. Most of the things that happened in your lifetime is a function of decision.

Decisions are the gateway into our freedom, liberty and a glorious future. When you settle for less, you can only get what is entitled for the less privilege. (See Luke 16:21). *"Despite all the riches of the father, the prodigal son took a drastic decision that reduced him to eat the pig's food, until he came to himself."* (Luke 15:17) Although you might not have noticed nor considered these, your lifestyle is wrapped up in the decisions you make.

HOW TO ACTIVATE THE HOLY SPIRIT IN YOUR LIFE

First of all, you must believe that there is a Holy Spirit.

1) ***Acknowledge*** the person of the Holy Spirt.

2) ***Believe*** in the ministration of the Holy Spirit.

3) ***Submit & obey*** the person of the Holy Spirit.

4) ***Welcome*** the sweet presence of the Holy Spirit.

Begin a relationship with the Holy Spirit today and make Him your best friend. Never start your day without inviting the person of the Holy Spirit to come into your life.

SUMMARY OF CHAPTER ONE

Prayer is **listening** and **talking** to **God** in a **dialogue**. It is **communicating** to the **Spirit of God**.

So many of us PRAY all the time without getting results—although too many Bible scholars have made so many definitions about **praying in the spirit**.

All access into praying in the spirit is by the help of the Holy Spirit. If the Holy Ghost grants you utterance, then we can pray in the spirit.

Likewise, the Spirit also helpeth our infirmities. *"For we know not what we should pray for as we ought: but the Spirit itself maketh intercession for us with groanings which cannot be uttered."* (Romans 8:26)

It takes the conviction of the Holy Ghost to pray in the spirit. Praying in the spirit confuses the devil. When we pray in the spirit, it is the Holy Spirit that is in control. Praying in the spirit is higher than praying in English. We must always allow the Holy Spirit to be in control when we pray in the spirit.

Praying in the spirit grants greater results. Praying in the spirit, coupled with fasting, brings down the anointing of God.

*Is any among you afflicted? Let him pray. Is any merry?
Let him sing Psalms. Is any sick among you?
Let him call for the elders of the church;
and let them pray over him, anointing him
with oil in the name of the Lord: And the prayer
of faith shall save the sick, and the Lord shall
raise him up; and if he have committed sins, they shall
be forgiven him. Confess your faults one to another, and
pray one for another, that ye may be healed. The effectual fervent prayer of a righteous man availeth much.*
James 5:13-16

Praying in the spirit is so vital that it not only heals us, but it also attacks the devil from his unknown position. Every time we pray in the spirit, the devil is confused. When we pray in English or another known language, everyone that understands that language knows what we are saying. But when we pray in the **spirit**, we speak mysteries.

*For he that speaketh in an unknown tongue
speaketh not unto men, but unto God:
for no man understandeth him;
howbeit in the spirit he speaketh mysteries.*
1 Corinthians 14:3

DECISION KEYS

1) Nothing changes until you make up your mind.

2) Decision is the gateway to deliverance.

3) Until you decide, no one will decide for you.

4) Your prosperity is proportional to your decisions.

5) The decision you make will determine the future you will create

6) Decision creates future and fulfills destinies.

7) Decision beautifies our future.

8) Decision keeps you out of trouble.

9) Decision exempts you from evil.

10) Decision gurantees eternity.

11) You can only go far in life by your faith decisions.

12) You are poor because you made such decisions

13) Make a decision and change your life.

14) Life changing decisions are a function of quality

information.

15) Success in life is a function of decision.

16) Life experiences are full of decisions.

17) Decisions change destinies.

18) Never settle for information—always look for revelation.

19) You are where you are today based on your last decision.

20) Information is crucial in decision making.

21) Decision makers rule the world.

22) You can rule your world with quality decisions.

23) As long as you decide rightly, Satan cannot harrass you.

CHAPTER 2
THE TONGUE OF ANGELS

Though I speak with the tongues of men and of angels, and have not charity, I am become as sounding brass, or a tinkling cymbal
1 Corinthians 13:1

Praying in the spirit means speaking in another language. That language is the tongue of ANGELS.

For he that speaketh in an unknown tongue speaketh not unto men, but unto God: for no man understandeth him; howbeit in the spirit he speaketh mysteries.
1 Corinthians 14:2

Every time we genuinely speak in tongues while **praying in the spirit**, we provoke the **angels of the Lord** to intervene on our behalf in the Earth realm. *"For if I pray in an unknown tongue, my spirit prayeth, but my understanding is unfruitful. What is it then? I will pray with the spirit, and I will pray with the understanding also: I will sing with the spirit, and I will sing with the understanding also."* (1 Corinthians 14:14-15)

Ministering **Spirit** is released to **fight** our battles—especially when we **call upon** them while **praying in the spirit**. *"Let them be as chaff before the wind: and let the angel of the Lord chase them. Let their way be dark and slippery: and let the angel of the Lord persecute them."*

(Psalms 35:5-6)

But to which of the angels said he at any time, Sit on my right hand, until I make thine enemies thy footstool? Are they not all ministering spirits, sent forth to minister for them who shall be heirs of salvation?
Hebrews 1:14

Whenever we PRAY IN THE SPIRIT, it is the HOLY GHOST who controls our tongue. *"Likewise the Spirit also helpeth our infirmities: for we know not what we should pray for as we ought: but the Spirit itself maketh intercession for us with groanings which cannot be uttered."* (Romans 8:26)

Call unto me, and I will answer thee, and show thee great and mighty things, which thou knowest not.
Jeremiah 33:3

We can genuinely receive great and mighty things when we PRAY IN THE SPIRIT from the desired perspective. Our PRAYER will never be fruitful until we understand how to PRAY and get results IN THE SPIRIT. *Therefore I say unto you, What things soever ye desire, when ye pray, believe that ye receive them, and ye shall have them.* (Mark 11:24)

Lets's briefly examine the HOLY GHOST:

THE HOLY SPIRIT IS THE UNQUENCHABLE FIRE

I indeed baptize you with water unto repentance. But he that cometh after me is mightier than I, whose shoes I am not worthy to bear: he shall baptize you with the Holy Ghost, and with fire:
Whose fan is in his hand, and he will throughly purge his floor, and gather his wheat into the garner; but he will burn up the chaff with unquenchable fire.
Matthew 3:11-12

The Holy Spirit is the anointing of God. You may ask why?

Because the Spirit of the Lord rests upon the anointing.

> *But ye have an unction from the Holy One, and ye know all things.*
> **1 John 2:20**
> **(also see 1 Samuel 16:13-14)**

THE HOLY SPIRIT IS THE REFINERS FIRE

Behold, I will send my messenger,
and he shall prepare the way before me:
and the Lord, whom ye seek, shall suddenly come
to his temple, even the messenger of the covenant,
whom ye delight in: behold, he shall come,
saith the Lord of hosts. But who may abide
the day of his coming? and who shall stand
when he appeareth? for he is like a refiner's fire,
and like fullers' soap: And he shall sit as
a refiner and purifier of silver: and he shall
purify the sons of Levi, and purge them
as gold and silver, that they may offer
unto the Lord an offering in righteousness.
Malachi 3:1-3

THE HOLY SPIRIT IS THE REFINERS FIRE

For the law of the Spirit of life in Christ Jesus
hath made me free from the law of sin and death.
Romans 8:2

HIGHLIGHTS TO ACTIVATE THE WORKS OF THE HOLY SPIRIT

PURIFICATION

Without sanctification and purification, we cannot PRAY and get results. The HOLY SPIRIT as the unquenchable fire does a quick and a swift work. John 9:31 says, *"God heareth not sinners."* In my interpretation, the Holy Spirit ignores all sinners. Sanctification is the platform for the works of the Holy Spirit.

As long as there is sin in your life, the Holy Spirit will not manifest through you and in you.

QUICKENING POWER

It is the HOLY SPIRIT who will quicken your tongue, especially while PRAYING. *But if the Spirit of him that raised up Jesus from the dead dwell in you, he that raised up Christ from the dead shall also quicken your mortal bodies by his Spirit that dwelleth in you.* (Romans 8:11)

CONDITION TO RECEIVE THE HOLY SPIRIT

REPENTANCE

Although the HOLY GHOST assures us with "RESTORATION," genuine REPENTANCE is the access code to SPEAK IN TONGUES, THE LANGUAGE OF THE ANGELS. *Repent and be baptized every one of you in the name of Jesus Christ for the remission of sins, and ye shall receive the gift of the Holy Ghost.* (Acts

2:38)

BE BAPTIZED

Whenever we are truly baptized in the HOLY GHOST, we operate on the next level dimension of life. *Be baptized every one of you in the name of Jesus Christ for the remission of sins, and ye shall receive the gift of the Holy Ghost.* (Acts 2:38)

CONFESSION OF OUR SINS

Genuine confession is the key to our total deliverance. We are told in Proverbs 28:13, *"He that covereth his sins shall not prosper: but whoso confesseth and forsaketh them shall have mercy." If we confess our sins, he is faithful and just to forgive us our sins, and to cleanse us from all unrighteousness.* (1 John 1:9)

ACKNOWLEDGMENT

We must acknowledge that we are sinners, and that Jesus Christ died for your sins. (Romans 3:23)

BORN AGAIN

We must be born again. It is impossible to pray in the spirit without experiencing genuine salvation (new birth).

Jesus answered and said unto him, Verily, verily,

*I say unto thee, Except a man be born again,
he cannot see the kingdom of God. Nicodemus saith unto
him, How can a man be born when he is old? can he enter
the second time into his mother's womb, and be born? Jesus
answered, Verily, verily, I say unto thee, Except a man be
born of water and of the Spirit, he cannot enter into the
kingdom of God. That which is born of the flesh is flesh;
and that which is born of the Spirit is spirit. Marvel not that
I said unto thee, Ye must be born again. The wind bloweth
where it listeth, and thou hearest the sound thereof, but canst
not tell whence it cometh, and whither it goeth: so is every
one that is born of the Spirit.*
John 3:3-8

CHAPTER 3
THE FORCES OF THE SPIRIT

These few forces of the Spirit must be in place if we must prevail, praying in the spirit. The force of faith, the mystery of the blood of Jesus, the name of Jesus Christ, the power and mystery of righteousness, the mystery of purity and sanctification, joy and praise and the power of love.

FAITH

Holding the mystery of the faith in a pure conscience.
1 Timothy 3:9

Faith is a force of the Spirit that frustrates the desire of the devil. If we must pray in the spirit correctly, we must engage the mystery of faith greatly. Praying in the spirit is not complete unless we engage the mystery of faith. Faith is a primary force of the Spirit that strengthens our praying in the spirit. *But without faith it is impossible to please him: for he that cometh to God must believe that he is, and that he is a rewarder of them that diligently seek him.* (Hebrews 11:6)

THE BLOOD OF JESUS

And they overcame him by the blood of the Lamb, and by the word of their testimony; and they loved not their lives unto the death..
Revelation 12:11

The blood of Jesus is our last weapon to pull the trigger over the head of the devil. Every time we pled **the blood of Jesus** while **praying in the spirit**, we blast the head of the serpent—the devil. **The blood of Jesus Christ** is our intercontinental ballistic missile for the demise of the devil. Colossians 1:13 says, *"Who hath delivered us from the power of darkness, and hath translated us into the kingdom of his dear Son."*

THE NAME OF JESUS CHRIST

The name OF JESUS is our power of the attorney. Jesus as our advocate pleads our case before the righteous judge. *"Wherefore God also hath highly exalted him, and given him a name which is above every name: That at the name of Jesus every knee should bow, of things in heaven, and things in earth, and things under the earth; And that every tongue shall confess that Jesus Christ is Lord, to the glory of God the Father."* (Phillipians 2:9-11)

THE POWER & MYSTERY OF RIGHTEOUSNESS

He that doeth righteousness is righteous, even as he is righteous.
1 John 3:7

And who is he that will harm you, if ye be followers of that which is good?
1 Peter 3:13

As long as we practice **righteousness**, we remain perpetually free from the wiles and schemes of the devil. **Righteousness** is the foundation for **praying in the spirit**. We **dominate** and **overpower** the devil every time we stand in the position of **righteousnes while praying in the spirit**.

THE MYSTERY OF PURITY & SALVATION

Unto the pure all things are pure: but unto them that are defiled and unbelieving is nothing pure; but even their mind and conscience is defiled.
Titus 1:15

The realms of the SPIRIT are like a physical courtroom. At every hearing of our case, it is the mystery of purity and sanctification that sets us free from the accusation of the wicked devil. Purity and sanctification are forces of the spirit that deliver speedily—especially when we PRAY IN THE SPIRIT.

JOY OF THE LORD

Joy and praise are FORCES OF THE SPIRIT that deliver at the platform of understanding. *"For God is the King of all the earth: sing ye praises with understanding."* (Psalms 47:7) The Bible tells me that **the joy of the Lord is our strength**. *"Neither be ye sorry; for the joy of the Lord is your strength."* (Nehemiah 8:10) As long as we cultivate a praiseful and joyful lifestyle, we easily impeach and frustrate the devil when we PRAY IN THE SPIRIT.

Apostle Peter defined the mysteries and attributed this joy as "joy unspeakable full of glory." *"Whom having not seen, ye love; in whom, though now ye see him not, yet believing, ye rejoice with joy unspeakable and full of glory."* (1 Peter 1:8) *"Thou wilt shew me the path of life: in thy presence is fulness of joy; at thy right hand there are pleasures for evermore."* (Psalms 16:11)

FASTING

Among the **forces of the spirit** that displace the devil is **fasting**. Fasting displaces the devil in a manner that the wicked devil cannot recover. Every time we fast and pray we, without reservation, yield the member of our body to compulsory subjection under the power of the Holy Ghost. If you are on a medication, consult with your **Pastor** before you go for longer periods of **fasting**. Fasting is a strong force of the SPIRIT that without argument defeats the devil any time.

THE POWER OF LOVE

The power of love for God and the kingdom of God is a powerful mystery that puts us at an advantage over the token of the devil. God knows our level of love towards him. That is why every time we pray in the Spirit and call upon him, he responds speedily to all his lovers. The Bible says, *"for God so LOVED, he gave..."* (John 3:16) Every time you love, it is confirmed by your ability to give. The love here is that love that makes faith to work. *"...but faith which worketh by love."* (Galatians 5:6) *"And hope maketh not ashamed; because the love of God is shed abroad in our hearts by the Holy Ghost which is given unto us."* (Romans 5:5)

WALKING IN LOVE

For our **praying in the spirit** to be effective and efficient, we must walk in LOVE with GOD. The reason GOD blessed Solomon beyond measures was because he LOVED THE LORD with all his heart. *"And Solomon loved the Lord, walking in the statutes of David, his father: only he sacrificed and burnt incense in high places."* (1 Kings 3:3) **Love is one of the forces of the Spirit that gurantees endurance, strength, patience and might.** Although Job suffered great devastation, he did not change his mind concerning his GOD. Job said, *"Though he slay me, yet will I trust in him: but I will maintain mine own ways before him."* (Job 13:15)

Then said his wife unto him, Dost thou still retain thine integrity? Curse God, and die.
Job 2:9

Even when Job's wife encouraged him to curse God and die, Job said, *"For I know that my redeemer liveth, and that he shall stand at the latter day upon the earth."* (Job 19:25) We can lose everything else, but not our LOVE for God and His Kingdom. *"But he knoweth the way that I take: when he hath tried me, I shall come forth as gold."* (Job 23:10) Job's victory came as a result of His LOVE for GOD and the Kingdom of GOD.

WHO WILL THE HOLY GHOST HELP IN THE SPIRIT?

But the manifestation of the Spirit is given to every man to profit withal.
1 Corinthians 12:7

The Holy Spirit always helps us while **praying in the spirit**—especially when we have a combination of these attributes.

1) THE MEEKNESS
2) THE HUMILITY

3) WISDOM TO FEAR THE LORD
4) THOSE WHO WALK IN LOVE & AGREEMENT
5) THE SPIRITUAL
6) THE RIGHTEOUS
7) THE FAITHFUL

Praying in the spirit is evidence to everyone that truly live in the spirit. *"If we live in the Spirit, let us also walk in the Spirit."* (Galatians 5:25) As long as we operate in the **spirit, praying in the spirit and getting powerful results are guaranteed**. *"For to be carnally minded is death; but to be spiritually minded is life and peace."* (Romans 8:6) *"But the natural man receiveth not the things of the Spirit of God: for they are foolishness unto him: neither can he know them, because they are spiritually discerned."* (1 Corinthians 2:14) *"This I say then, Walk in the Spirit, and ye shall not fulfil the lust of the flesh."* (Galatians 5:16)

HOW DO I LIVE IN THE SPIRIT?

Turn you at my reproof: behold, I will pour out my spirit unto you, I will make known my words unto you.
Proverbs 1:23

We must recognize the person and presence of the holy ghost in our life.

We must obey and yield to the leading of the holy ghost in our lives.

We must always pray and fast often.

WHAT THE LORD HATES

These six things doth the Lord hate: yea, seven are an abomination unto him:
A proud look, a lying tongue, and hands that shed innocent blood,
An heart that deviseth wicked imaginations, feet that be swift in running to mischief,
A false witness that speaketh lies, and he that soweth discord among brethren.
Proverbs 6:16-19

We must reco

HINDRACE TO RECEVING THE HOLY SPIRIT

BITTERNESS

It is impossible for us to **pray genuinely in the Spirit** as long as our SPIRIT man is BITTER. *"Looking diligently lest any man fail of the grace of God; lest any root of bitterness springing up trouble you, and thereby many be defiled."* (Hebrews 12:15)

INIQUITY

Acquaint now thyself with him, and be at peace: thereby good shall come unto thee. Receive, I pray thee, the law from his mouth, and lay up his words in thine heart. If thou return to the Almighty, thou shalt be built up, thou shalt put away iniquity far from thy tabernacles. Then shalt thou lay up gold as dust, and the gold of Ophir as the stones of the brooks.
Job 22:21-24

As far as I know, only dogs return to its own vomit. Iniquity—which literally means the repetition of the sin that easily beset us—separates us from the **Spirit of the Lord—the Holy Ghost.** *"But your iniquities have separated between you and your God, and your sins have hid his face from you, that he will not hear."* (Isaiah 59:2)

UN-FORGIVENESS

As long as we do not forgive others, we cannot genuinely **pray in the spirit**. Praying in the spirit-it means praying in the language of the Holy Ghost. *"Wherefore I say unto you, All manner of sin and blasphemy shall be forgiven unto men: but the blasphemy against the Holy Ghost shall not be forgiven unto men."* (Matthew 12:31)

REGRET

If we must pray genuinely in the spirit, we must be conscious of our mindset. Our reason for praying and fasting must be righteous before God. We must be open-minded, willing to help the needy. Always ready to share and be loving to all our loved ones—even to strangers.

A great man once said, "When you are depressed, you are living in the past, when you are anxious you are living in the future, but when you are at PEACE you are living in the present." *"Remember ye not the former things, neither consider the things of old. Behold, I will do a new thing; now it shall spring forth; shall ye not know it? I will even make a way in the wilderness, and rivers in the desert."* (Isaiah 43:18-19)

So many **religious folks** live in **regret** all their lives, feeling envy towards others who are doing well in lives. When we live in **regret**, we **frustrate the power and presence of the holy ghost**.

Remember it is the HOLY GHOST who helps our infirmities. *"Likewise the Spirit also helpeth our infirmities: for we know not what we should pray for as we ought: but the Spirit itself maketh intercession for us with groanings which cannot be uttered."* (Romans 8:26)

We will not be able to PRAY IN THE SPIRIT and get results, especially if we hold on to memories of past troubles, lost opportunities and failed careers.

What are we saying?

PRAY IN THE SPIRIT

When we **pray in the spirirt,** we are not speaking to men but unto GOD. *"For he that speaketh in an unknown tongue speaketh not unto men, but unto God: for no man understandeth him; howbeit in the spirit he speaketh mysteries."* (1 Corinthians 14:2)

Every time we **genuinely pray in the spirit, we overcome the devil**. As long as we speak in tongues, we put the devil into confusion—especially when we pray in the language of the angels. *"And suddenly there came a sound from heaven as of a rushing mighty wind, and it filled all the house where they were sitting. And there appeared unto them cloven tongues like as of fire, and it sat upon each of them. And they were all filled with the Holy Ghost, and began to speak with other tongues, as the Spirit gave them utterance."* (Acts 2:2-4)

CONCLUSION OF CHAPTER 3

We must apply all the forces of the SPIRIT if we desire to get anything out of our PRAYERS. As a BELIEVER, with the accreditation of a **spiritul law enforcement officer**, armed with the warrant for the **arrest of the devil**, every time we **pray in the spirit**, we not only frustrate the devil, but we put him into the bottomless pit of hell—"sheol" in Hebrew.

The devil is scared every time strong believers **pray in the Spirit with all the forces of the Spirit.** If we must overcome the wicked one—the devil—we must be strong in the realms of the spirit.

"Put on the whole armour of God, that ye may be able to stand against the wiles of the devil. For we wrestle not against flesh and blood, but against principalities, against powers, against the rulers of the darkness of this world, against spiritual wickedness in high places. Wherefore take unto you the whole armour of God, that ye may be able to withstand in the evil day, and having done all, to stand. Stand therefore, having your loins girt about with truth, and having on the breastplate of righteousness; And your feet shod with the preparation of the gospel of peace; Above all, taking the shield of faith, wherewith ye shall be able to quench all the fiery darts of the wicked. And take the helmet of salvation, and the sword of the Spirit, which is the word of God: Praying always with all prayer and supplication in the Spirit, and watching thereunto with all perseverance and supplication for all saints." (Ephesians 6:11-18)

CHAPTER 4
THE HELP OF THE HOLY SPIRIT

Likewise the Spirit also helpeth our infirmities: for we know not what we should pray for as we ought: but the Spirit itself maketh intercession for us with groanings which cannot be uttered.
Romans 8:26

Regardless of how we define it, the Holy Spirit is our comforter and our helper any day. He is an **advocate and a representative** of the supreme soversign power of God. As a caretaker and representative, He helps us in every area of our lives. *"For in him we live, and move, and have our being; as certain also of your own poets have said, For we are also his offspring."* (Acts 17:20)

*I will lift up mine eyes unto the hills,
from whence cometh my help.
My help cometh from the Lord,
which made heaven and earth.*
Psalms 121:1-2

As long as we understand how the Holy Spirit works and operates, we will never suffer a nervous breakdown, depression or heart attack. We must totally surrender and depend on HIM. Jesus made it clear to us all, *"These things I have spoken unto you, that in me ye might have peace. In the world ye shall have tribulation:*

but be of good cheer; I have overcome the world."

If you are now a born again Christian, fire baptized, speaking in tongue and in the Holy Ghost, it does not exempt you from experiencing life challenges. As believers, we have the privilege to acquaint our lives with the help of the Holy Spirit. (See John 14:18, 26) We have the accreditation as spiritual law enforcement officers to evict demons far away from our lives. *"And whatsoever ye shall ask in my name, that will I do, that the Father may be glorified in the Son. If ye shall ask any thing in my name, I will do it."* (John 14:13-14)

GODLY Wisdom demands that—

"What you do not want, you don't watch."
"What you do not resist has power to remain."
"What you don't confront, you can't conquer."

These few quotes are the solution to every challenge you will ever encounter in life. Most of our shortcomings are an inability to confront challenging situations.

WHO WILL THE HOLY GHOST HELP IN PRAYERS?

THE BORN AGAIN BELIEVER
We do not have a chance to provoke the Holy Ghost unless we confess the LORD Jesus as our savior and REPENT of our sins. We established earlier that

the Holy Spirit does not lead sinners. The Spirit of the Lord becomes a reality upon our lives when we confess Jesus Christ as our Lord and savior.

"Jesus answered and said unto him, Verily, verily, I say unto thee, Except a man be born again, he cannot see the kingdom of God. Nicodemus saith unto him, How can a man be born when he is old? can he enter the second time into his mother's womb, and be born? Jesus answered, Verily, verily, I say unto thee, Except a man be born of water and of the Spirit, he cannot enter into the kingdom of God. That which is born of the flesh is flesh; and that which is born of the Spirit is spirit. Marvel not that I said unto thee, Ye must be born again. The wind bloweth where it listeth, and thou hearest the sound thereof, but canst not tell whence it cometh, and whither it goeth: so is every one that is born of the Spirit." (John 3:3-8)

Until we confess and acknowledge the Lord Jesus as our savior, we will forever be subdued with trials and tribulation. The most important reason we must be born again is for our SOUL to make HEAVEN. *"For what shall it profit a man, if he shall gain the whole world, and lose his own soul? Or what shall a man give in exchange for his soul?"* (Mark 8:36-37)

THE FEAR OF GOD

And unto man he said, Behold, the fear of the Lord, that is wisdom; and to depart from evil is understanding.
Job 28:28

We must develop the consciousness of the fear of God in our heart if we desire the help of the HOLY GHOST. *"The fear of the Lord is the beginning of wisdom: and the knowledge of the holy is understanding."* (Proverbs 9:10)

As long as we fear God, the help of the Holy Spirit is on the way. The Lord made it clear things shall be well with the righteous, but they shall not be well with the wicked.

Though a sinner do evil an hundred times, and his days be prolonged, yet surely I know that it shall be well with them that fear God, which fear before him: But it shall not be well with the wicked, neither shall he prolong his days, which are as a shadow; because he feareth not before God.
Ecclesiastes 8:12-13

The Holy Spirit teaches us all things as long as we undertsand the fear of God in our life. *"The fear of the Lord is the beginning of wisdom: a good understanding have all they that do his commandments: his praise endureth forever."* (Psalms 111:10)

What man is he that feareth the Lord? him shall he teach in the way that he shall choose.
Psalms 25:12

BOLDNESS
As long as we desire to **pray in the spirit**, we

must be bold about it. We must always be bold to speak to God in the language that the devil does not understand. *"Let us therefore come boldly unto the throne of grace that we may obtain mercy, and find grace to help in time of need."* (Hebrews 4:16) Every believer has the accreditation by the blood of Jesus to exercise boldness in all area of our lives.

Until we put up the spirit of boldness to **pray in the spirit**, we will not be able to communicate effectively in the **realms of the spirit**. I admonish you to gather courage and boldness and **pray in the spirit like never before**. *"And when they had prayed, the place was shaken where they were assembled together; and they were all filled with the Holy Ghost, and they spake the word of God with boldness."* (Acts 14:31)

AUTHORITY

Every **man/woman of the spirit, is a man/woman of authority**. Often times we forget that **the holy ghost is present to help us in our prayers**. *"Nevertheless I tell you the truth. It is expedient for you that I go away: for if I go not away, the Comforter will not come unto you; but if I depart, I will send him unto you."* (John 16:7) *"Then he called his twelve disciples together, and gave them power and authority over all devils, and to cure diseases."* (Luke 9:1) If we must **pray in the spirit** we must operate with AUTHORITY in order to EVICT THE DEVIL out of our lives and affairs.

HAVE FAITH IN GOD

It is inevitable to PRAY effectively IN THE SPIRIT without HAVING FAITH IN GOD. *"But without faith it is impossible to please him: for he that cometh to God must believe that he is, and that he is a rewarder of them that diligently seek him."* (Hebrew 11:6) Recall—*"When a man's ways please the Lord, he maketh even his enemies to be at peace with him."* (Proverbs 16:7)

WE MUST BE IN AGREEMENT WITH THE HOLY SPIRIT

Praying in the spirit demands agrement with the holy ghost. *"Can two walk together, except they be agreed?"* (Amos 3:3)

ENDURANCE

The stronghold to overcome the wicked devil is the **spirit of endurance**. As much as we **pray in the spirit**, we must be able to endure persecution, hardship and difficulty.

Apostle Paul once said, *"Of the Jews five times received I forty stripes save one. Thrice was I beaten with rods, once was I stoned, thrice I suffered shipwreck, a night and a day I have been in the deep; In journeyings often, in perils of waters, in perils of robbers, in perils by mine own countrymen, in perils by the heathen, in perils in the city, in perils in the wilderness, in perils in the sea, in perils among false brethren; In weariness and painfulness, in watchings often, in hunger and thirst, in fastings often, in cold and nakedness.*

And ye shall be hated of all men for my name's sake: but he that endureth to the end shall be saved." (Matthew 10:22)

BE MEEK

It takes MEEKNESS to PRAY feverently in the SPIRIT. Every man/woman of the SPIRIT is a man/woman of MEEKNESS. We are always exalted in life with the attribute of humility. Let this mind be in you, which was also in Christ Jesus: *"Who, being in the form of God, thought it not robbery to be equal with God: But made himself of no reputation, and took upon him the form of a servant, and was made in the likeness of men: And being found in fashion as a man, he humbled himself, and became obedient unto death, even the death of the cross. Wherefore God also hath highly exalted him, and given him a name which is above every name."* (Phillippians 2:5-9) *"The meek will he guide in judgment: and the meek will he teach his way."* (Psalms 25:9)

If we must overcome the wicked devil, we must be meek before our god and before all men. *"But he giveth more grace. Wherefore he saith, God resisteth the proud, but giveth grace unto the humble. Submit yourselves therefore to God. Resist the devil, and he will flee from you."* (James 4:6-7) *"He hath put down the mighty from their seats, and exalted them of low degree."* (Luke 1:52)

PRAYER POINTS TO OVERCOME TRIALS BY THE HELP OF THE HOLY SPIRIT

1) Father Lord, deliver me from this present trial, in the name of Jesus.

2) Almighty Father, break me out of this present obscurity, in the name of Jesus.

3) Holy Spirit, help me to overcome this trial, in Jesus name.

4) Holy Spirit, speak to me, in the name of Jesus.

5) Holy Spirit, minister to my subconscious spirit, in the name of Jesus.

6) Fire of God, burn down every mountain of difficulty, in the name of Jesus.

7) Holy Ghost, baptize me with your fire, in the name of Jesus.

8) Holy Spirit, go before me and favor me in this present challenge, in the name of Jesus.

9) Spirit of God, grant me liberty and freedom by the fire of the Holy Spirit, in the name of Jesus.

10) Father Lord, intervene on my behalf, in the name of Jesus.

11) Ancient of day, liberate me this season, in the name of Jesus.

12) Immortal redeemer, bring me higher above these prevailing changes.

13) Lord God, turn this present obstacale into my miracle, in the name of Jesus.

14) Fire of God, break down these obstacles for me, in the name of Jesus.

15) Holy Spirit, favor me in, Jesus name.

16) Holy Spirit. release me from this challenge, in the name of Jesus.

17) Holy Spirit, become my compionion, in Jesus name.

18) Holy Spirit, represent me in this matter.

19) Holy Spirit, elevant me beyond my own immagination, in the name of Jesus.

20) Holy Spirit, do not allow my enemies to truimph over my life, in the name of Jesus.

21) Fire of God, protect me, in the name of Jesus.

22) Fire of God, destroy my enemies, in the name

of Jesus.

23) Fire of God, build a wall around me, in the name of Jesus.

24) Fire of God, expose my enemies, in the name of Jesus.

25) Fire of God, prove yourself, in the name of Jesus.

26) Holy Spirit, represent me in jesus name.

27) Holy Spirit, release your boldnes into my life.

28) Holy Spirit, grant me signs and wonders.

29) Holy Spirit, make me a living wonder in my lifetime.

30) Holy Spirit, turn my life around, in the name of Jesus.

31) Holy Spirit, I will not remain at this level, in the name of Jesus.

32) Spirit of God, lift me higher, in the mighty name of Jesus.

33) Angels of God, minister unto me, in the name of Jesus.

34) Hand of God, separate me this season, in the name of Jesus.

CONCLUSION

We must always have a prayer life if we must make heaven.

And he spake a parable unto them to this end, that men ought always to pray, and not to faint.
Luke 18:1

We must understand that **praying in the spirit** is the **language of the angels**. Mysteries are released every time we genuinely **pray in the spirit.**

For he that speaketh in an unknown tongue speaketh not unto men, but unto God: for no man understandeth him; howbeit in the spirit he speaketh mysteries.
1 Corinthians 14:3

For I fear, lest, when I come, I shall not find you such as I would, and that I shall be found unto you such as ye would not: lest there be debates, envyings, wraths, strifes, backbitings, whisperings, swellings, tumults
2 Corinthians 12:20

"We MUST REPENT OF OUR SINS!"

This book will not help you make heaven without genuine repentance.

Have you accepted the lord Jesus Christ?
Our salvation must be sure. We must be saved to make heaven. Eternity is real!

Therefore if any man be in Christ, he is a new creature: old things are passed away; behold, all things are become new.
2 Corinthians 5:17

Now repeat this prayer after me:

Say Lord Jesus, I accept you today, as my Lord and my savior. Forgive me of my sins, wash me with your blood. Right now, I believe I am sanctified, I am saved, I am free. I am free from the power of sin, to serve the Lord Jesus. Thank you Lord for saving me. Amen.

Congratulations. You are now...

A BORN AGAIN CHRISTIAN.

Again I say to you—CONGRATULATIONS!

What must I do to determine my divine visitation?

To determine divine visitation you must be born again! The word says as many as received him, to them gave He power to become the sons of God. Even to them that believe on his name.

To qualify for divine visitation, do the following sincerely:

1) Acknowledge that you are a sinner and that He died for you. (Romans 3:23)

2) Repent of your sins. (Acts 3:19, Luke 13:5, 2 Peter 3:9)

3) Believe in your heart that Jesus died for your sin. (Romans 10:10)

4) Confess Jesus as the Lord over your life. (Romans 10:10, Acts 2:21)

NOW REPEAT THIS PRAYER AFTER ME:
Say Lord Jesus, I accept you today, as my Lord and my savior, forgive me of my sins wash me with your blood. Right now, I believe, I am sanctified, I am save, I am free, I am free from the Power of sin to serve the Lord Jesus. Thank you Lord for saving me. Amen.

Congratulations.

YOU ARE NOW A BORN AGAIN CHRISTAIN!

Again, I say to you—congratulations!

I adjure you to watch the Spirit of God bear witness with your Spirit confirming His word with signs following. The word says the Spirit itself beareth witness with our spirit, that we are the children of God. Join a bible believing church or join us on our weekly and Sunday worship services at 343 Sanford Avenue Newark New Jersey 07106.

HEALING KEYS

1) Always carry a positive mindset, regardless of the prevailing circumstances.

2) Always tell yourself the truth before you lie about it.

3) If the truth be told, you are a branch of His blessings, the planting of the Lord.

4) Never confess that you are sick to the hearing of the member of your body.

5) Positive confession with faith yields positive results.

6) Every cures of man have no power to prevail over your life.

7) A merry heart is medicinal and health to your body.

8) Spiritual and emotional well-being is vital to happiness in life.

9) To avoid depression, never have regrets.

10) Never be anxious in life to avoid anxiety.

11) Always live today for today to be at peace with your spirit and with God.

11) You're unique because your challenges are tailored

to you only.

12) The blessing always dominates the curses any day.

13) Decisions are the wheels of life.

14) We either ride into fame or into shame.

15) Daily exercise and some reading of the Bible gurantees good health.

16) Every day is God's day. No day created by God is a disapointment.

17) Stay away from sweet stuff—they are temporary.

18) Sugar is sweet to your taste, beware! It also contributes to diabetes.

19) A good prayer life gurantees longivity.

20) People that pray in tongues do not develop mental disease.

21) Always be positive in everything.

22) Always have a mentor in life that will oppose and fight the tormentor.

23) Always have someone in life to learn from.

24) Tell everybody what you plan to do and someone will help you do it.

25) Winners fight to the last.

26) Quitters never win in life.

27) Soul winners are heirs to the kingdom of god.

28) Soul winners never lack help.

29) Soul winners are cerified with divine help.

30) God is always looking for soul winners to bless.

31) Life is a warfare and not a funfare.

32) In life you fight for all you possess.

33) No man or woman was born rich.

34) In your lifetime do something positive to impact your world.

35) Take care of your life today—you don't have one to spare.

36) Take your life serious before the devil take you down.

37) Always be cheerful at all times.

38) Regardless of the prevailing circumstances around you, your life is in the hand of God.

39) God is the super surgeon that will spiritually-surgically heal you.

40) Always expect help from above and not from abroad.

41) Man will disappoint you, but god will appoint you.

42) The joy of the lord is always our strength.

43) Spiritual height is not measured in length or breath.

44) If you go deeper with God, you will see deeper.

45) Your next level in life is full of recognition.

46) Go to where you are celebrated and not where you are tolerated.

47) Develop yourself in the area of your calling in life.

48) A lifestyle of thanks given keeps God 24/7 on duty on our behalf.

49) Develop a lifestyle of thanksgiving.

50) Thanksgiving gurantees our access to obtain the promises.

WISDOM KEYS

— Every productive society is a society heading to the top.

—Millions of Nigerians run away from Nigeria. Very few Nigerians stay in Nigeria.

—My decision to return Nigeria is the will of God for my life.

—My shortcoming in America after 18 years is the fact that I've trained me to be wise, to think, reflect and reason appropriately.

—If you train your mind to reason, it will train your hands to earn money.

—It is absurd to use the money of the heathen to build the kingdom of the living God.

—Every ministry reveals its agenda and VISION either at the beginning or at the end.

—Be careful of your life. It is your first ministry.

—The average American mind is conditioned for a continual quest to get new things and discard the old.

—When I considered well, my BMW jeep became my initial deposit for the work of the ministry in Nigeria.

—Money will never fall from any tree or person. Make up your mind to be independent today.

—Everyone is waiting for you to change your mind. Until you change your thinking, nothing changes around you.

—Multiple academic degrees in other disciplines gave me the chance to think and reason.

—Whatever anyone is thinking at any time reveals what is inside of their heart.

—All planned events are the product of meditation.

—Every event is designed for a designated timeline.

—Wisdom is your ability to think, to create and invent.

— If you can think wisely enough, you will come out of debt.

—The distance between you and your success is your innovative and creative ability to think well.

—Success is the result of hard work, commitment, resolve and determined learning from past mistakes and failings.

—If you organize your mind, you have organized your life and destiny.

—There is a thin line between success and failure.

—Wealth is your ability to think, power is your ability to reason and success is your ability to be informed.

—If you can make use of your mind by thinking and reasoning, God will make use of your life and destiny.

—Reflect, reason, think and be Great.

—Famous people are born of woman.

—That you will make it is your intention, that you will survive is your resolve, that you will succeed with changes is your determination, personal efforts and hard work.

—No man was born a failure.

—Lack of vision is the result of failure.

—Working with mental patients encourages and aspire me to be a productive observant and dedicated to my assignment.

—Successful people are not magicians. It is the willpower, combined with hard work and determination and a resolve to succeed, that make them succeed.

—In the unequivocal state of the mind, intention is not a location or a position. It is the state of the mind.

—So many people think that they think.

—The mind is used to think, to reflect and to reason.

—You will remain blind with your eyes open until you can see with your mind by thinking.

—There is no favoritism in accurate and precise calculation.

—Although knowledge is power, information is the key and gateway to a great future.

—It will take the hand of God to move the hand of man.

—With the backing of the great wise God, nothing will disconnect you from your inheritance.

—As long as you have wisdom and understanding of God, Satan and evil cannot manipulate your life and destiny.

—You have come this far in life by your own judgment and the decisions you made in the past. Now lean in and listen to God for another dimension of greatness.

—Great people are ordinary people. It is extra ordinary efforts and the price of sacrifice that produces greatness in them.

—As a mental direct care worker, I saw a great pastor and a motivational speaker within myself.

—A menial job does not reduce your self-worth. Until you resolve to achieve greatness and see greatness in all you do, you will never count in your community.

—The principle of Jesus will solve your gambling and addiction problems.

—The man of Jesus will lead you into heaven.

—Everyone has their self-appraisal and what they think about you. Until you discover yourself, other opinions about you will alter the real you.

—Supervisors and directors are just a position in the chain of command in a workplace. Never allow your supervisor hierarchy to alter your opinion of yourself.

—Everyone can come out of debt if they make up their mind.

—The fact that I am not a decision-maker at work does not diminish my contribution to my world.

—Although it appears like it was a poor decision to accept a direct care employment at a psychiatric hospital, as I reflect on my nine years of that experience, it became apparent that I have learned and experienced enough for my next assignment.

—Self-encouragement and determination is a resolve of the heart.

—If you are determined to make a difference and do the things that make a difference, you will eventually make a difference.

—Good things do not come easy.

—Short cuts will cut your life short.

—Those who look ahead move ahead.

—Life is all about making an impact. In your lifetime strive to make an impact in your community.

—Make friends and connect with people who are moving ahead of you in life.

—If you can look around well, you have come a long way in your life, made a lot of difference and realized a lot of success in life.

—If you are my old friend, hurry up to reach out to me before I become a stranger to you.

—I am blessed with inspirations from God that changed my interpretation of the world around me.

—I thought I was stagnant and lonely until I looked around and noticed my children running around and my wife cooking.

— At 40, I resigned my job to seek the Lord forever.

—My ministry took a drastic rise to the top when the wisdom of God visited me with knowledge and understanding.

—You will be a better person if you understand the characteristics of your personality like your mood swings, attitudes and habits.

—It is the seed of love you sow into the heart of a child and a woman that you reap in due time.

—Love is not selfish. Love shares everything, including the concealed secrets of the mind.

—As long as you have a prayer life and a Bible, you will never feel lonely in the race of life.

—When good friends disconnect from you, let them go. They might have seen something new in a different direction.

—Confidence in yourself and in God is the only way to bring you out of captivity

—Never train a child to waste his or her time.

—The mind is the greatest asset of a great future.

—You walk by common sense, run by principles and fly by instruction.

—Those who become successful in life did it by self-determination, hard work and learning from past failures.

—Most successful people are lonely people. No one renders help to them, believing they are already successful. Except when they seek for more knowledge and information, they are all alone.

— I have seen a towing truck vehicle. I have also seen a towing ship in the water. But I have never seen a towing airplane in the air.

—I exercise my judgment and make a decision every minute of the day. Decisions are crucial, critical and vital with reference to your future.

—So many people wish for a great future. You can only work towards a great future.

—Your celebrity status began when you discovered your talent. What are you good at? Work at it with all your commitment.

—Prayers will sustain you, but the wisdom of God will prosper you.

—When I met Oyedepo, his teachings changed my perspective. But when I met Ibiyeomie, his teachings changed my perception.

— I will be successful in ministry if only I concentrate and focus my energy in the work of the ministry.

— It took the late Dr. Norman Vincent Peale's book to open my mind towards the kingdom of success.
—You walk by common sense, run by principles and fly by instruction.

CHAPTER 5
PRAYER OF SALVATION

I am glad you have read this book all the way from the beginning to this point. All I have said from the beginning will remain a mystery until you commit it into practice.

And before you do so, I want you, if you have not given your life to Jesus, to do so now. Give your life to Christ. I want you to know the truth! The truth is that Jesus died for your sins. And because He died, you must be alive and prosperous

What must I do to determine my divine visitation? To determine divine visitation you must be born again!

The word says as many as received Him, to them gave He power to become the sons of God. Even to them that believe on His name. To qualify as a BORN AGAIN CHRISTIAN you must sincerely—

1) Acknowledge that you are a sinner and that He died for you. (Romans 3:23)

2) Repent of your sins. (Acts 3:19, Luke 13:5, 2 Peter 3:9)

3) Believe in your heart that Jesus died for your sins. (Romans 10:10)

4) Confess Jesus as the Lord over your life. (Romans 10:10, Acts 2:21)

Now repeat this prayer after me:

Say Lord Jesus, I accept you today, as my Lord and my savior. Forgive me of my sins, wash me with your blood. Right now, I believe I am sanctified, I am saved, I am free. I am free from the power of sin, to serve the Lord Jesus. Thank you Lord for saving me. Amen.

Congratulations. You are now...

A BORN AGAIN CHRISTIAN.

Again I say to you—CONGRATULATIONS!

I adjure you to watch the Spirit of God bear witness with your Spirit, confirming His word with signs following. The word says The Spirit itself beareth witness with our spirit, that we are the children of God.

MIRACLE CARE OUTREACH

*"...But that the members should have
the same care one for another"*
1 Corinthians 12:25

    We are all members of the body of Christ. Jesus commanded us to love our neighbor as ourselves. This includes caring for one another as a member of one body. True love is expressed in caring and giving. The word says, for God so Love He gave....

    Reach out to someone in need of Jesus. Help someone in crisis find Christ. Look out and prove your love to Jesus by caring and inviting your friends and associates to find Jesus the Healer.

    Invite your friends to our Home Care Cell Fellowship (Miracle Chapel Intl. Satellite Fellowship). We're in the U.S. at 33 Schley Street, Newark, New Jersey 07112. Home Care Cell Fellowship Group meets every Tuesday at 6:00pm-7:00pm.

    If you are in Nigeria—MIRACLE OF GOD MINISTRIES, aka "MIRACLE CHAPEL INTL." Mpama–Egbu-Owerri Imo state Nigeria.

LIFE IS NOT ALL ABOUT DURATION, BUT IT'S ALL ABOUT DONATION

What does this statement mean?

Life consists not in accumulation of material wealth. (Luke 12:15) But it's all about liberality…i.e., what you can give and share with others. (Proverbs 11:25) When you live for others, you live forever—because you outlive your generation by the legacy you leave behind after you depart into glory to be with the Lord. But when you live for yourself, when you are reduced to SELF—you are easily forgotten when you die and depart in glory.

Permit me to admonish you today to live your life to be a blessing to a soul connected to you today. I want you to know that so many souls are connected and looking up to you, and through you so many souls will be saved and rescued from destruction. Will you disciple someone today to find Jesus Christ?

As a genuine Christian, it is your duty to evangelize Jesus Christ to all you meet on your way. Jesus is still in the healing business—Jesus is still doing miracles, from time of old to now. Therefore, tell someone about Jesus Christ today, disciple and bring them to Church. *Philip findeth Nathanael...* (John 1:45)

Please prove the sincerity of your love for God today, please become a soul winner. The dignity of your Christianity is hidden in your boldness to proclaim and evangelize Jesus Christ to all you meet on your way. There is a question mark on the integrity of your Christianity until you become a life soul winner. Invite someone to join us worship the Lord Jesus this coming Sunday. Amen.

MIRACLE OF GOD MINISTRIES
PILLARS OF THE COMMISSION

We Believe, Preach and Practice the following:

1) We believe and preach Salvation to every living human being.

2) We believe and preach Repentance and Forgiveness of sins.

3) We believe and preach the baptism of the Holy Spirit and Spiritual gifts.

4) We believe and teach Prosperity.

5) We believe and preach Divine Healing and Miracles—Signs and Wonder.

6) We believe and preach Faith.

7) We believe and proclaim the Power of God (Supernatural).

8) We believe and proclaim Praise and Worship to God.

9) We believe and preach Wisdom.

10) We believe and preach Holiness (Consecration).

11) We believe and preach Vision.

12) We believe and teach the Word of God.

13) We believe and teach Success.

14) We believe and practice Prayer.

15) We believe and teach Deliverance.

These 15 stones form the Pillars of Our Commission.
Become part of this church family and follow this great move of God.

MY HEARTFELT PRAYER FOR YOU

It is my burning desire for God to touch you through one of our teaching books or CDs. It also my personal desire for you encounter God for yourself.

Now let me Pray for you:

O Lord God! I beseech thee, and through personal prayer intercession today that the Holy Spirit will touch the precious soul reading this book and turn their life around. Spirit of God, possess this loved one. Lord, overcome all dominating, controlling forces that have prevailed over their lives. I come against all oppressive thought, in Jesus name. Henceforth, I pronounce you free from manipulation, intimidation and domination of the wicked enemy called the devil. You are free from all satanic harassment and assaults. Amen.

TIME TO TURN TO GOD

You must be SAVED!

It is time to receive our lord Jesus Christ as your personal savior. *"For what shall it profit a man, if he shall gain the whole world, and lose his own soul? Or what shall a man give in exchange for his soul?"* (Mark 8:36-37)

You must change the way you live. Come out of sin before it destroys your whole life and destiny. Change the way you relate to others. As long as you are willing to **repent**, God is willing to restore your life.

Have you ever asked why are you here? God planted you here to bring to pass his plan over your life. Eternity is real, heaven is sure. Become interested in the heavenly race and book your name in the lamb book of LIFE.

Everything great comes by his grace upon your life. Therefore, turn unto God in suplication, in thanksgiving and in prayer, and God will turn in your favor.

ABOUT THE AUTHOR

Rev. Franklin N. Abazie is the founding and Presiding Pastor of Miracle of God Ministries, with headquarters in Newark, New Jersey USA and a branch church in Owerri-Imo State Nigeria. He is following the footsteps of one of his mentors, the healing evangelist Oral Roberts of the blessed memory. The Lord passed Oral Roberts' healing mantle two days before he went to be with the Lord at age 91 into the hands of healing evangelist Rev. Franklin N. Abazie in a vision.

In all his services, the Power and Presence of God is present to heal all in his audience. Rev. Abazie is an ordained man of God, with a Healing Ministry reviving the healing and miracle ministry of Jesus Christ of Nazareth.

Pastor Franklin N. Abazie, has been called by God with a unique mandate: **"THE MOMENT IS DUE TO IMPACT YOUR WORLD THROUGH THE REVIVAL OF THE HEALING AND MIRACLE MINISTRY OF JESUS CHRIST OF NAZARETH.**

"I AM SENDING YOU TO RESTORE HEALTH UNTO THEE AND I WILL HEAL THEE OF THY WOUNDS, SAID THE LORD OF HOST"

Rev. Abazie is a gifted, ardent teacher of the word of God, who operates also in the office of a

Chapter 6 — About the Author

Prophet, generating and attracting undeniable signs and wonders, special miracles and healings, with apostolic fireworks of the Holy Ghost. He is the founding and presiding senior Pastor of this fast growing Healing Ministry. He has written over 86 inspirational, healing and transforming books covering almost all aspects of divine healing and life. He is happily married and blessed with children.

BOOKS BY REV. FRANKLIN N. ABAZIE:

1) The Outcome of Faith
2) Understanding the Secret of Prevailing Prayers
3) Commanding Abundance
4) Understanding the Secret of the Man God Uses
5) Activating My Due Season
6) Overcoming Divine Verdicts
7) The Outcome of Divine Wisdom
8) Understanding God's Restoration Mandate
9) Walking In the Victory and Authority of the Truth
10) God's Covenant Exemption
11) Destiny Restoration Pillars
12) Provoking Acceptable Praise
13) Understanding Divine Judgment
14) Activating Angelic Re-enforcement
15) Provoking Un-Merited Favo
16) The Benefits of the Speaking Faith
17) Understanding Divine Arrangement
18) How to Keep Your Healing
19) Understanding the Mysteries of the Speaking Faith
20) Understanding the Mysteries of Prophetic Healing
21) Operating Under the Rules of Creative Healing
22) Understanding the Joy of Breakthrough
23) Understanding the Mystery of Breakthrough
24) Understanding Divine Prosperity
25) Understanding Divine Healing
26) Retaining Your Inheritance
27) Overcoming Confusing Spirit
28) Commanding Angelic Escorts

MIRACLE OF GOD MINISTRIES

NIGERIA CRUSADE 2012

MIRACLE OF GOD MINISTRIES
NIGERIA CRUSADE
2012

MIRACLE OF GOD MINISTRIES
NIGERIA CRUSADE 2012

MIRACLE OF GOD MINISTRIES

NIGERIA CRUSADE

2012

MIRACLE OF GOD MINISTRIES

NIGERIA CRUSADE

2012

www.ingramcontent.com/pod-product-compliance
Lightning Source LLC
Chambersburg PA
CBHW021446080526
44588CB00009B/714